DISCARDED

DAILY LIFE

The Great Depression

Peggy J. Parks

KIDHAVEN
PRESS™

THOMSON
———————™
GALE

San Diego • Detroit • New York • San Francisco • Cleveland
New Haven, Conn. • Waterville, Maine • London • Munich

For more information, contact
KidHaven Press
27500 Drake Rd.
Farmington Hills, MI 48331-3535
Or you can visit our Internet site at http://www.gale.com

LIBRARY OF CONGRESS CATALOGING-IN-PUBLICATION DATA

Parks, Peggy J., 1951-
  The Great Depression / by Peggy J. Parks.
    p. cm. — (Daily life)
Summary: Portrays daily life in America between the world wars, from the excite-
ment of the "Roaring Twenties," through the devastation of the stock market
crash and drought, to the New Deal and economic recovery.
Includes bibliographical references and index.
ISBN 0-7377-1399-2 (alk. paper)
    1. United States—History—1933–1945—Juvenile literature. 2. Depressions—1929—
United States—Juvenile literature. 3. United States—History—1919–1933—Juvenile
literature. 4. United States—Economic conditions—1918-1945—Juvenile literature.
[1. United States—History—1933-1945. 2. United States—History—1919–1933.
3. Depressions—1929. 4. United States—Social life and customs—1918–1945. 5. New
Deal, 1933–1939.] I. Title. II. Series.
  E806.P3555 2004
  973.917—dc21
                                                                    2003009410

Contents

CHAPTER ONE

Exciting Times

The 1920s were exciting times in America. World War I had ended in 1918, and people were relieved that the country was at peace. Factories that had made military equipment started making automobiles. In 1910 there were five hundred thousand cars in America, and by 1920 there were over 8 million. As more people bought cars, factories were needed to build them. That meant more jobs and the highest wages that had ever been paid.

Americans were confident about the future. They had money to spend and they were eager to spend it. They bought new homes and luxury items such as radios, washing machines, refrigerators, and vacuum cleaners. They also bought electric phonographs and records to play on them. They flocked to theaters each week to watch silent films that starred popular actors such as Charlie Chaplin, Mary Pickford, and Rudolph Valentino. They danced the Charleston and fox-trot in music halls. In this decade known as the "Roaring Twenties," Americans enjoyed the highest standard of living in the world.

Ownership in Companies

Americans also used their money to buy **stocks**, which were individual **shares** of businesses. These shares were a form of agreement between stockholders and companies

Two women dance the Charleston on the edge of a roof. The 1920s were happy times for most Americans.

that sold stock. By purchasing shares, buyers were lending money to companies. As companies made money, they agreed to pay part of it back to stockholders in the form of **dividends**.

People were encouraged to invest in American businesses. The author of the book *A Nation in Torment* describes the attitude most people had about investing in stocks during the 1920s: "Get ahead! Make the most of your life! . . . Bet on the future of America!"[1] Investing in companies that owned factories was considered patriotic. Plus investing in the **stock market** was a chance to get rich. Many people invested their entire life savings.

To make stocks more affordable, and make it easier for people to buy more shares, investors were allowed to buy **on margin**. That meant they were only paying a small percentage of the selling price rather than the full amount. For example, those who wanted to buy ten thousand dollars worth of stock only had to pay one thousand dollars. Their **stockbrokers**, whose job was to buy and sell stocks, paid the difference by borrowing from banks.

The Stock Market Booms

As people invested money in American companies, stocks became more valuable. So prices kept climbing higher. Between 1923 and 1929 the combined average price of American stock increased by 176 percent.

Some companies experienced huge increases in their stock prices. One example was the Radio Corporation of America (RCA), which was the biggest producer of radios. People depended on radios for music,

A family listens to the news on the radio. Stock in radio companies was very valuable in the late 1920s.

sporting events, comedy programs, and news. Radio sales boomed and that caused RCA stock to jump in value. In just six months during 1929, the stock price rose from less than one hundred dollars per share to over five hundred dollars per share. This happened with other businesses as well.

In some cases, however, stock prices went up for no apparent reason. This was mostly the result of **pooling**, which was a secret agreement between large investors to control stock prices. Investors pooled their money to buy large quantities of a company's stock. As more shares of stock were sold, the price went up—which made the stock seem to be worth more than it really was. Smaller investors, who knew nothing about pooling, mistakenly believed that the stock had become more valuable. So they bought it too, which caused the price to climb even more. When the stock was at a high enough price, the pooling investors sold their shares. This resulted in huge profits for them, but it made the price of the stock drop. The unsuspecting smaller investors lost money when that happened.

Stockbrokers read the bad news about falling stock values. The stock market collapsed on October 29, 1929.

Signs of Trouble

If only a few people had engaged in pooling, it would not have made much difference. That was not the case, though. Thousands of investors bought and sold stocks this way, which caused stock prices to rise and fall unexpectedly.

On September 3, 1929, the stock market reached its highest point. Because it had been climbing for so long, people were overconfident. They believed it would continue to rise, maybe forever. Some, however, began to fear that America was headed for a crisis. They became nervous about their investments. During September and October people started selling their stocks to avoid losing money. Suddenly everyone was selling instead of buying. This sent the stock market into a sharp, downward spiral.

The Beginning of the End

On October 24, 1929, a day that is known as "Black Thursday," a chain of events led to the stock market's collapse. As the value of stocks continued to drop, investors became more frightened. Bankers were nervous because they had loaned millions of dollars to brokers for stock purchases. They started making margin calls, which were demands for borrowers to pay back more of the money that was owed on their stocks.

People who bought on margin often did so because they could not afford the full stock price. So they did not have money to repay their loans. Their only choice was to sell their stocks and salvage whatever they could. As more investors sold, stock prices fell even further. By 11:00 A.M. on October 24, prices were dropping by the minute

A young man who lost his savings in the stock market crash sells his car for a fraction of its worth.

and people started to panic. Now everyone wanted to sell stock at any price. The problem was they could not sell because no one was buying. By midafternoon, stock values had shrunk by more than 10 billion dollars.

Things seemed as though they could not get worse, but five days later they did. Stock prices kept falling—and falling, and falling. **Wall Street**, the New York City financial district where stocks were traded, was like a war zone. Brokers were doing everything possible to sell stocks. Outside the New York Stock Exchange, people collapsed in shock and grief. Hundreds of police officers tried to control mobs of frantic investors.

By 5:30 P.M. on October 29, when the day's trading had stopped, over 30 billion dollars in investments was gone. The stock market had crashed. October 29, 1929, would forever be known as "Black Tuesday."

America was stunned. For so long there had been nothing but hope and excitement in the country. Now the future looked uncertain and bleak. People's life savings were gone. They owed money they could never repay. The prosperous Roaring Twenties were a thing of the past and the entire nation was gripped in fear.

CHAPTER TWO

A Devastated Country

A fter the stock market disaster, American banks were in trouble. The millions of dollars they had loaned— for stocks, homes, cars, and other purchases—would likely go unpaid. All over the country people heard rumors that banks were on the verge of closing.

Americans began to panic and rushed to withdraw their money from banks. In an effort to avoid losing all their assets, the banks tried to keep people out. Author Gene Smith describes a typical scene:

> At the banks the depositors jostled for places in line, and the police had to get rough while wondering if they themselves would have a payday that week . . . [W]omen came to demand their money and, finding their bankbooks worthless, fell to beating with their hands on the locked plate-glass doors. They screamed through the night for their money, but when no one came out to give it to them, they went away.[2]

In 1930 a total of 1,326 banks closed their doors. Then, on December 11, 1930, New York's Bank of the

United States collapsed. It was one of the largest banks in the country. When it failed, more than a million people lost their savings. Americans had not only lost faith in the stock market. Now they no longer trusted banks.

Bleak Times

The stock market crash and bank failures were like a giant snowball rolling out of control. Americans, who

Children march with signs urging a factory owner to rehire their dad. Factories laid off thousands of workers after the stock market crash.

had splurged freely for ten years, stopped spending money on houses, cars, and other products. Factories laid off thousands of workers. Businesses, which had grown rapidly during the 1920s, were now forced to close, causing thousands more to lose their jobs. Banks continued to collapse. America was in the clutches of the Great Depression.

Herbert Hoover, the president of the United States, encouraged people not to give up hope. He believed the problems were temporary and that prosperity would return in a matter of months. Yet the situation was grow-

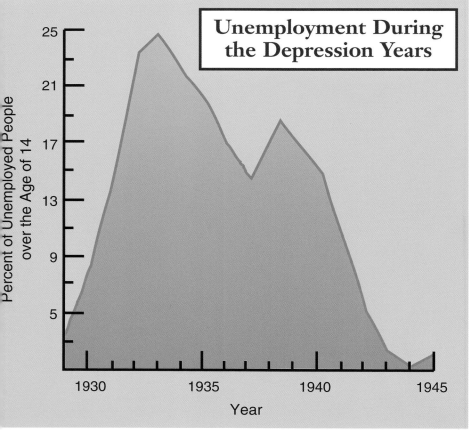

Unemployment During the Depression Years

Percent of Unemployed People over the Age of 14

Year

Source: Historical Statistics of the United States, Colonial Times to 1970.

ing worse, not better. Businesses all over the country were failing. By mid-1930, of the 125 million people in America, more than 8 million were out of work. One year later that number had jumped to 13 million.

As people continued to lose their jobs, many had no money to buy food. Thousands of people stood in line to get free food from churches, the Salvation Army, and other charitable organizations. Often these **breadlines** were several city blocks long. By 1931 breadlines existed in cities and towns all over America.

One Family's Story

Millions of families suffered through hard times during the Great Depression. Earl Wheeler was a child then, but he has vivid memories of how tough things were. In 1930 his father lost his job at a Lansing, Michigan, automobile factory after working there for fifteen years. With a wife and three children to support, he was desperate to find work. Finally, he found a job at a shop that fixed dents in car fenders. It was fifty miles away and the place only needed him a few days a week, but he was still relieved to have the job.

Wheeler describes what his family went through:

I remember that we barely had any food. After working for the first three days, Dad came home with his paycheck and he found that our house was **quarantined** because I had scarlet fever. That meant we couldn't go out and he couldn't come in. He bought us groceries and had to leave them on the front porch, and he talked to us through

Unable to make ends meet during the Great Depression, people waited in breadlines for hours to get free food.

the window. After the quarantine was over, Mom could finally get out so she went and stood in a line to get food for us.

Wheeler says things were bad, but his parents were thankful for a place to live. "We were living in a rented house and we couldn't afford the rent. Our landlord was kind enough to let us live there for free. Later, when Dad finally found another job, we paid a little extra each month until we were caught up." [3]

Plight of the Homeless

Wheeler's family struggled because of the depression, but they were more fortunate than many others. Hundreds of thousands of people had no place to live. Those who could no longer afford their mortgage payments lost their homes. Apartment dwellers who could not pay their rent were forced to move out. Homelessness had become a major crisis.

Homeless people lived anywhere they could find shelter. Some families stayed in abandoned buildings, under bridges, or even in their cars. Dorothy Bell, who lived on an Illinois farm during the depression, remembers one family who had lost their home. They had nowhere to go so they lived in their car. After driving for

This family lost everything and was forced to move into a tent. Homelessness became a huge problem during the depression.

many miles so the father could hunt for work, they showed up at her family's door. She explains:

> I shudder to think about it . . . There were three children. My father couldn't afford to hire the father, but he found something for the man to do for a couple of hours. Of course we gave him lunch . . . My mother had chocolate cake, in addition to the sandwiches. The man said that he was going to take his piece out to his children. My mother said you mean that your children had no dinner? . . . So my mother packed a lunch of sandwiches and milk. When father paid him, mother then gave them the cake. They had had no breakfast, either. [4]

Hoovervilles

Some homeless people built shacks to live in. **Shantytowns**, or clusters of shacks, sprang up all over America. They were made of whatever materials people could find—packing crates, scraps of wood, sheets of tin, bricks and stones, and even abandoned cars. These makeshift communities were found in almost every state. In Seattle, Washington, hundreds of shantytowns were located near rivers and railroad tracks. New York City also had many shantytowns, the largest of which was in Central Park.

Americans could see no end to the Great Depression, and most of them blamed Herbert Hoover. They believed the president should be able to do something to end their misery. Because of the bitterness people

Shantytowns like this one in Colorado sprang up in every state. Homeless people built shacks out of any available material.

felt toward Hoover, shantytowns throughout the country were called "Hoovervilles."

No End in Sight

By 1932 nearly 15 million people had no jobs. Millions of Americans had lost their homes or apartments and had no place to live. Families lacked food and could not afford health care or medicine. Hundreds of schools closed because they did not have the money to operate. People were angry, ashamed, and afraid. In a country that was long known as the land of opportunity, all that remained was hopelessness and despair.

CHAPTER THREE

A Cruel Trick of Nature

When the Great Depression struck America, most people suffered. Yet one group of people was hit especially hard—the farmers. They had prospered during World War I because there was a great demand for products such as wheat and corn. When the war ended the demand for these products dropped. Farmers were forced to lower their crop prices. At the same time they had to pay higher costs for farming supplies and equipment. So they went deeper into debt, and many lost their farms to the banks that had loaned them money.

A Devastating Drought

The farmers who managed to hold onto their land felt fortunate. They continued to grow crops and raise livestock such as pigs, sheep, and cattle. Because America's farmland was fertile and rich, these farmers could usually make a decent living. Then, in the summer of 1931, the rains stopped. For months the sun blazed from a cloudless sky, baking the earth and everything that grew. Entire fields of crops withered and died. Thousands of acres of lush grass, trees, and shrubs became scorched and brown. Ponds and streams dried up, and rivers disappeared. Still there was no sign of rain.

Farmers had experienced dry spells in the past, but nothing like this. Of all the states that were affected by

Many farmers, like those seen here, lost their farms during the Great Depression.

"LANDLESS"

The Dust Bowl and the Dispossessed

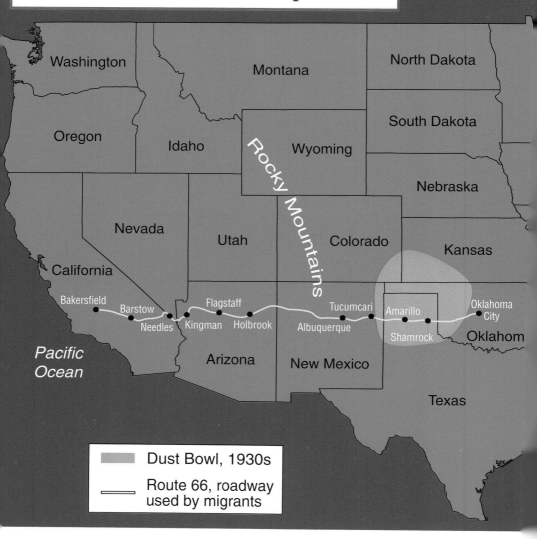

Dust Bowl, 1930s

Route 66, roadway used by migrants

the 1931 **drought**, the Great Plains states of Oklahoma, Kansas, Texas, Colorado, and New Mexico suffered the most. Their fields had been overgrazed by livestock, and many people had used careless farming practices. They had plowed the fields so much that the land was overused and damaged. So as the drought dragged on, the rich, black topsoil that once carpeted the fields dried up and turned to dust.

Black Blizzards

People in the Great Plains were used to seeing **whirlwinds** in the hot, dry summer months. These small, swirling masses of air gathered dust as they skittered along the ground. Early in the summer of 1931, no one noticed that the whirlwinds seemed larger and stronger than in the past. At first it was not obvious that they were picking up more dust and moving much faster than usual.

Without warning, forceful winds began to roll across the land with a thunderous roar. With no vegetation to keep the topsoil in place, the winds picked up the powdery dirt and formed enormous black clouds. Sometimes the clouds completely blocked the sun, causing towns to be dark in the daytime. The nights were pitch-black because neither the stars nor the moon could pierce the shroud of dust.

When people saw these "black blizzards," they were terrified. Many thought it was the end of the world. J.R. Davison, who lived on his parents' farm in the 1930s, explains how it felt to watch the massive dirt clouds approaching: "We could see this low cloud bank . . . You could see it all the way across. And we watched that thing and it got closer. Seemed to kind of grow you know and it was getting closer. The ends of it would seem to sweep around. And you felt like . . . you were surrounded. Finally, it would just close in on you. Shut off all the light. You couldn't see a thing."[5] When the winds finally died down, fences, machinery, trees, and even farm animals were buried under mounds of dirt. Sometimes people could not get out of their doors because the dirt drifts were as high as the roof. Fields had become useless for farming. Yet the black blizzards raged on, sometimes lasting for days or weeks.

During the storms people had no way to escape. They could not go outside because the dust blinded them, and it choked them so they could not breathe. When they were inside, nothing could keep the dust out. People soaked sheets and towels with water and stuffed them into the cracks of doors and windows. Still the dust seeped through tiny crevices and covered every surface in their homes, forming black ridges on the floor. Dust was in the air, the food, and the water.

A man and his children seek shelter from a black blizzard. Such storms were common in the Great Plains states.

People could not keep from breathing it, and the dust coated their lungs and made them sick.

It seemed as though the drought and dust storms would never end. In 1932 fourteen storms occurred, and the next year there were nearly three times as many. A journalist visiting the Great Plains in 1935 nicknamed it the "dust bowl."

On April 14, 1935, a day known as "Black Sunday," history's worst black blizzard struck. After a brief period of blue skies, the temperature suddenly dropped and the storm rolled in. A magazine writer later described it: "People caught in their own yards grope for the doorstep. Cars come to a standstill, for no light in the world can penetrate that swirling murk . . . The nightmare is deepest during the storms. But on the occasional bright day and the usual gray day we cannot shake from it. We live with the dust, eat it, sleep with it . . . The nightmare is becoming life."[6]

A Desperate Journey

By the end of 1935, millions of acres of land were destroyed and countless farmers had lost their farms. Thousands of people had died from heat and dust-related illnesses. Nature had plagued the Great Plains for nearly five years, and no one knew how long it would continue.

Some people decided they could take no more. After farming the land for decades, they had lost everything. So more than three hundred thousand Great Plains farmers and their families packed their belongings into

Out of work, Oklahoma farmers walk to California. The billboard on their right advertises the comfort of traveling by train.

battered cars and trucks. They abandoned their farms and slowly headed west to California. They had heard it called the Golden State, a place where lush fields of orchards, cotton, and grapes stretched for miles. They believed it was their last chance to find a better life.

Once they had made the thousand-mile trip, however, they found that life in California was just as hard as the lives they left behind. People sneered at them, calling them "Okies" (for Oklahoma, which was particularly hard hit by dust storms). The word meant poor and uneducated and dressed in ragged clothes. If they were able to find work picking cotton or grapes, they were often paid less than fifty cents for an entire day. They lived in tents and shacks, and many died from hunger or disease.

Hope at Last

The people who chose to stay and cling to their farms wondered how long they could hold on. Throughout the summer of 1939, the drought and dust storms continued. Farmers began to doubt whether it would ever rain again. Then in the autumn a miracle happened—the rains began to fall.

After eight years of drought, the farmers of the Great Plains states were relieved to see the rains of 1939.

One man, whose family managed to save their farm, describes the relief people felt when the rain came: "It meant life itself. It meant a future. It meant that there would be something better ahead of you. And . . . you'd go out in that rain and just feel that rain hit your face. It was a—a very emotional time when you'd get rain because it meant so much to you. You didn't have false hope anymore, you knew then that you was going to have some crops."[7]

The rain did not mean that hard times were over for farmers. They still had to struggle with damaged land, debt, and low crop prices. However the drought had ended and the winds had finally stopped blowing. After eight years of devastation, people once again had a reason to hope.

CHAPTER FOUR

From Ruin to Recovery

As America struggled with the effects of the Great Depression, a new president vowed to take action. In November 1932 the people elected Franklin Delano Roosevelt to the nation's highest office. When he gave his first speech on March 4, 1933, he spoke these famous words: "Let me assert my firm belief that the only thing we have to fear is fear itself."[8] He made it clear that he was the people's president, and that his priority was to work toward healing the country's problems.

The New Deal

The task Roosevelt faced was anything but easy. At the time he took office, the depression had reached its worst point. Businesses continued to go bankrupt. Unemployment was in the millions. Nearly 40 percent of the people lived in poverty. Of the twenty-five thousand banks in America, eleven thousand had failed. The nation's industrial output was half of what it had once been. Farmers all over the country struggled to hold on to their land, and many had lost their farms.

President Roosevelt's administration designed posters like this one to inspire confidence in his New Deal plan to lift America out of the depression.

Unlike Hoover, Roosevelt felt that it was the government's duty to help solve the country's problems. He believed the government should spend money on programs that would help people. His solution was the **New Deal**, which he believed would bring relief, recovery, and reform to America. During the first hundred days of his presidency, he began to address the country's most pressing needs. With the support of Congress, he passed a number of laws. These were designed to reduce poverty, get people back to work, and boost the national economy.

Saving the Banks

Roosevelt knew that the bank closures were among the nation's biggest crises. Millions of Americans had lost their savings when the banks failed. People were still withdrawing money from the banks that remained open. If this continued, more banks would be forced to

President Roosevelt signs a bill to restructure the nation's banking system.

close. Within days after he was sworn in as president, Roosevelt declared a three-day "bank holiday." During this time he and his aides drafted the Emergency Banking Bill. This plan would close down banks that were broke and help repair and reopen banks that were strong enough to survive.

On March 12, 1933, Roosevelt talked to the American people in a national radio address. He announced that banks throughout the country were being investigated to make sure they were run properly. Some of them would begin to reopen the next day. He could not promise that every bank would reopen, or that there would be no more losses. He did promise, however, that the government would do everything possible to help. As Roosevelt had hoped, his speech restored people's confidence. Some banks reopened their doors and Americans who had money began depositing it again.

Helping the People

Soon after the president dealt with the bank crisis, he began working on another serious problem—the nation's unemployment. So many companies had gone bankrupt that hundreds of thousands of jobs had disappeared. As one way of putting people back to work, Roosevelt developed the Civil Conservation Corps. The program created 3 million government jobs, most of which were in national forests and parks. Workers dug ditches, planted trees, fought forest fires, and repaired trails. For their efforts they received thirty dollars per month and three meals a day.

Workers install a turbine at the Grand Coulee
Dam in Washington. The dam was built under the
Works Progress Administration program.

Roosevelt also created the Federal Emergency Relief
Act and an agency called the Federal Emergency Relief
Administration (FERA). Over the next two years, FERA
provided 3 billion dollars to states for programs to help
the poor.

Another New Deal program was the Works Progress
Administration (WPA). Set up in 1934, the WPA provided
jobs for millions of American men and women. For a
salary of about forty dollars per month, WPA workers

built hundreds of parks, dams, airports, hospitals, and schools. They also built more than seventy-five thousand bridges and a half-million miles of roads throughout America.

The Social Security Act, one of Roosevelt's most lasting programs, was passed in 1935. This legislation provided benefits for many people, including senior citizens and those who were blind or disabled.

Aid for Farmers

Roosevelt was also concerned about America's farmers. Soon after he became president, he approved a bill called the Agricultural Adjustment Act. This legislation paid farmers to grow less of certain crops. This, Roosevelt

Children play on the lawn of a home built with money from Roosevelt's programs to help the poor.

believed, would cause a natural increase in crop prices. Also, farmers who faced bankruptcy could ask for government loans.

The Soil Conservation Act was another New Deal program. The problems caused by the dust storms were partly because of careless farming. This program would give money to farmers who agreed to improve the way they planted and plowed. The Drought Relief Service helped poverty-stricken farmers by buying cattle from them, even if the animals were not healthy.

The People's President

Roosevelt's New Deal was designed to help the country recover from the Great Depression. His program saved America's banks and helped put people back to work. It also provided for the poor and helped feed the hungry. What it could not do, though, was make the nation's problems disappear. Several million people were still unemployed. Businesses continued their struggle for survival. Farmers were still plagued with high costs and financial ruin from years of drought. Thousands of families still remained homeless.

The New Deal did not cure America, but it did bring back the country's hope. People once again believed that a brighter future could be possible. They also had renewed faith in government because they admired and trusted Roosevelt. Since he had taken office, they had seen him keep his promises to work hard for the American people. They believed he was helping to make the country stronger. So, in 1936, they again elected him as their president.

Another World War

Three years after Roosevelt began his second term, the German dictator, Adolf Hitler, invaded Poland. World War II had begun. Japan and Italy became involved, as did Great Britain and France.

Roosevelt feared that the United States would also have to go to war. He wanted to warn the country. In a note he wrote to himself, he expressed his thoughts: "Unless some miracle beyond our present grasp changes the hearts of men, the days ahead will be crowded days—crowded with the same problems, the same anxieties that filled to the brim those September days of 1914 [World War I]. For history does in fact repeat." [9] A year later another election was held. Once again the American people elected Roosevelt as president.

The USS *Arizona* burns in Pearl Harbor, Hawaii.

A woman and a man work together at a defense factory. World War II created thousands of new factory jobs.

He had been in his third term of office for one year when America was attacked. On December 7, 1941, Japanese airplanes bombed the U.S. naval base at Pearl Harbor, Hawaii. The next day America declared war on Japan and entered World War II.

End of a Nightmare

In preparation for war American industry sprung to life. New factories opened to make airplanes and tanks. Other factories manufactured weapons, uniforms, and ammunition. Thousands of new jobs were created, and the nation's men and women were back to work. By

1943 less than 2 percent of the country's workforce was unemployed.

America had spent many years in the death grip of the Great Depression. The people had watched their country change from prosperous to poverty-stricken. They had suffered, they had struggled, and they had fought to survive. Now they finally had a new reason to believe in tomorrow.

Notes

Chapter 1: Exciting Times

1. Edward Robb Ellis, *A Nation in Torment: The Great American Depression 1929–1939.* New York: Coward-McCann, 1970, p. 27.

Chapter 2: A Devastated Country

2. Gene Smith, *The Shattered Dream.* New York: William Morrow, 1970, p. 55.
3. Earl Wheeler, interview with author, January 10, 2003.
4. Quoted in Sarah-Eva Carlson, "The Depression: Memories of a Farm Girl," *Illinois History,* May 1993, pp. 69–70.

Chapter 3: A Cruel Trick of Nature

5. Quoted in "An Eyewitness Account," *American Experience: Surviving the Dust Bowl,* PBS. www.pbs.org.
6. Quoted in "An Eyewitness Account," *American Experience: Surviving the Dust Bowl.*
7. Quoted in "An Eyewitness Account," *American Experience: Surviving the Dust Bowl.*

Chapter 4: From Ruin to Recovery

8. Franklin Delano Roosevelt, *First Inaugural Address,* March 4, 1933. www.pbs.org.
9. Quoted in Ellis, *A Nation in Torment,* p. 522.

Glossary

breadlines: The lines where people waited to get food from charitable organizations.

dividend: Money paid by a company to a person who bought stock.

drought: A long and severe lack of water because of no rainfall.

New Deal: Franklin Delano Roosevelt's program to help create jobs and decrease poverty.

on margin: Being allowed to pay a small amount of a stock's value rather than the total amount.

pooling: The secret practice of large investors that made stock prices go too high or drop quickly.

quarantine: Keeping a person or group away from other people because of a contagious disease.

shantytown: Clusters of shacks built by homeless people.

share: A unit of stock that forms an agreement between people who buy the stock and companies that sell it; when the companies make money, they agree to pay part of that money back to their stockholders in the form of dividends.

stock: Part ownership in a company.

stockbroker: Someone who buys and sells stocks for other people.

stock market: A general term for the system of buying and selling of stocks.

Wall Street: The financial district in New York City where stocks are bought and sold.

whirlwind: A swirling mass of air that picks up dust and debris as it moves along the ground (sometimes called a dust devil).

For Further Exploration

Books

Tricia Andryszewski, *Dust Bowl: Disaster on the Plains.* Brookfield, CT: Milbrook, 1993. A book about the devastating dust storms of the 1930s that turned much of the Great Plains into what was called the dust bowl.

Kerry A. Graves, *Going to School During the Great Depression.* Mankato, MN: Blue Earth, 2002. A book about what schools were like during the time of the Great Depression.

Robert J. Norrell, *We Want Jobs!: A Story of the Great Depression.* Austin, TX: Raintree Steck-Vaughn, 1993. Discusses the life of an unemployed Pittsburgh steelworker and his family during the tough times of the Great Depression.

Periodicals

"Every Silver Lining Has a Cloud," *Kids Discover,* August 2001, p. 16. An article about the stock market crash and other events of the 1920s.

"The Great Depression and the Dusty Thirties," *Crinkles,* November/December 2000, pp. 46–49. An informative article about the years of the depression and the dust bowl.

Ellen Whitford, "Rock Bottom," *Scholastic Update,* March 8, 1991, p. 16. An interesting article about the Great Depression that includes personal thoughts of people who remember it.

Websites

How Stuff Works: How Stocks and the Stock Market Work (http://money.howstuffworks.com).

Library of Congress Learning Page: Great Depression and World War II, 1929–1945 (http://memory. loc.gov).

New Deal Network (http://newdeal.feri.org).

PBS American Experience: Surviving the Dust Bowl (www.pbs.org).

PBS Kids, Learning Adventures in Citizenship: Wall Street and the 1929 Crash (www.pbs.org).

Index

Picture Credits

Cover Photo: © Hulton/Archive
© Bettmann/CORBIS, 7, 8, 10, 26, 27, 37
© CORBIS, 30, 36
Denver Public Library, Western History Collection,
  William L. Fick, call no. Z-2729, 19
Library of Congress, 16, 17, 24, 31, 34
© Minnesota Historical Society/CORBIS, 13
© Swim Ink/CORBIS, 21
© Underwood & Underwood/CORBIS, 5
U.S. Department of the Interior, 33

About the Author

Peggy J. Parks holds a bachelor of science degree from Aquinas College in Grand Rapids, Michigan, where she graduated magna cum laude. She is a freelance writer who has written a number of books for various Gale Group divisions, including KidHaven Press, Blackbirch Press, and Lucent Books. Parks lives in Muskegon, Michigan, a town that she says inspires her writing because of its location on the shores of Lake Michigan.